MONGANE WALLY SEROTE

LONGER POEMS
Third World Express
Come and Hope With Me

MAYIBUYE BOOKS
University of the Western Cape, Bellville

DAVID PHILIP PUBLISHERS
Cape Town Johannesburg

Mayibuye History and Literature Series No. 78

Longer Poems: Third World Express / Come and Hope With Me
first published in 1997 in southern Africa by David Philip Publishers
(Pty) Ltd, 208 Werdmuller Centre, Newry Street, Claremont, Cape,
South Africa, and Mayibuye Books, University of the Western Cape,
Bellville, Cape, South Africa

Third World Express (1992) and *Come and Hope With Me* (1994)
were first published separately by David Philip Publishers (Pty) Ltd

© Mongane Wally Serote 1997

ISBN 0-86486-351-9

All rights reserved. No part of this publication may be reproduced,
stored in a retrieval system, or transmitted in any form or by any
means, electronic, mechanical, photocopying, recording or otherwise,
without the prior permission of the publisher.

Printed and bound by Clyson Printers (Pty) Ltd, 11th Avenue,
Maitland, Cape Town, South Africa

MONGANE WALLY SEROTE

Third World Express

*"Just the other day at the Village Vanguard,
I heard Jackie and René McLean, father and son, play.
One of their songs was:
Third World Express."*

FOR THE BOYS
LENTSOE, ZWELI, SECHABA, VUYO AND THABO

THIRD WORLD EXPRESS

In the heart of this time
it is simple things which are forgotten,
desecrated
and defiled
they are fossilised into a past which is out of reach
ah
my friends
is it not a song or what we can share
is it not you and I
and all of us
who make things simple and magic
and that which is simple dazzle
tightening
like steel wire
or rope
or bone
or locomotive wheels
or fibre?
What is it we need!
a thought to share
about the bread we broke and together ate
a song we shared, which left magic in our hearts
in this time
it is simple things which we have forgotten
a glitter of your eye, telling me of your beauty
the smile of your face
which sparked mine into life
in the heart of this time
it is the simple things which are forgotten

remember
how as if life were an onion,
we sliced, and sliced and sliced it into tiny bits
lives
of babies, youth
we chopped and chopped and chopped as if we were
    preparing a meal!
On the streets of dust and debris
time
heavy with mud on its boots strides
its footprints and footsteps forever indelible on our eye,
how can you or I forget
the big things we did
like burning flesh
or
hacking life
or tearing it to ribbons with bombs
or poking neat black holes on foreheads of people,
how
how can you and I forget
or remember why we did it if
it is habit
or hatred
or greed
or callousness
or jealousy
how can we forget
how memory, like a mirror always reflects us
how
the sight of my eye on yours
and the sight of yours on mine can be indelible
how
your facial expression on mine
and mine on yours are a mirror
how
how do we forget such simple things!
look
take a look at where we are now

at this hour
how
a black child looks at a white child
or an African at an American
or an Asian at a Latin American
or
who
who are we at this hour
in this time
which is aged with its burden
mine and your interest
interest
what is it
my friends, what is it that is interest
a diamond which cannot be crushed
or gold
which can take what ever shape forever
is that what we have made of interest
interest
what is that —
not simple
nor anything to share
or magic
but greed and hatred
how
how did we come by this terrible finding
oh my friends tell me
how
how
if this earth
this air
this sky and sun
how
if all these we share or can share
how
how did we come to be here
in Iraq, where flesh and fire merge
or Pol Pot where skulls are packed neatly

3

as if they are eggs when they are white bones
and have holes they bare useful
or Bush
where to defy his interest can cost lives
lives
countless lives
maimed nations of orphans
how did we come here?
will a voice
as innocent as the little hand of a baby
be raised so I can see it
and hear it
like a song you and I can share
will a voice that innocent answer me
how
how did we come here, where we are!
there are good men
and there are good women in this time
where
where are they
in this place where some feed wild pigeons from their
 palms
while others spend sleepless nights thinking about stray
 dogs and cats
and others kill each other
are hungry now and forever
while others
tired of mansions go out camping
and others have nowhere to sleep —
by God
I know
there are good men and women —
in this place
and in this time the good are there!
they look you in the eye
in search
their faces are like still trees
and their shoulders are wide open

they wear tired eyes
they search and look
for what we can share
or for that moment which can make life magic
for that simple thing
for that, which can make *us* us!
they are black they are white
they share this earth with us
and their hearts are not steel
or gold
or stone
but are simple — flesh!
they are boers and blacks
women or men
they walk
like we do
and talk as we do
wonder with uncertainty like the sun paving clouds
but
something makes *them* them
good women and men
they are there
here
among us
they are sought;
elsewhere they are clubbed like dangerous snakes
somewhere else, they are lonely and caged
in this time
our time
in Paris they may speak French
and in Alexandra — what?
Zulu, Venda, Tsonga
or Sotho
elsewhere whatever
but they are single in tongue
to eliminate Aids
or
to seek to make us honest like science

or cherish the knowledge that conflict is part of life
and that life is life when it grows out of it
or
that time must be livable
or
how to rebuild houses into homes

These men and women are there
in this time utterly filled with silence and stealth
and in my country
where we bathe every second and minute in blood,
I wonder as I seek them
in time
and in sight, where they are
where are they that they cannot stop this carnage!
they try
we try
inch for inch
minute for minute
we try
how to stop blood which drowns the streets
how to say stop
how to make that simple word a deed
we try
as sharpened blades
and axes, flash and flash against the sunlight
slash flesh
crack skull
tear limb
and we attend mass burials, we try —
we seek and search
look
listen in the air for good men and women
and as we bury the dead
we try
to speak to Bush and his friends
even as we know that
the legless

the handless
and some who were not born blind
but are now blind
in Angola
in Mozambique
the earless and maimed
and the children who wash carnage blood from oranges
before they eat them
or walk dark nights hungry and lost
or hear death and see it walk in the footpaths
and at the hut whose door is as thin as paper
shaking in the winter night
and rattling from the footsteps of bandits,
we speak
since their life is speechless with terror
we speak
we plead at times
for in my country they are us
we speak in search of simple things
which can bind us miles apart to make us human
to make us share a magic moment
or song
which can say
since we share so much, can we not also share life?
Bush
we ask
where are the craftsmen of our time
where passengers in this time are passengers in adventure
we ask Savimbi
who for some is a writing on the wall startling the mind
we ask
where to now —
if knowledge creates the future
why
why can't we get ready!
I ask as if I was born yesterday
even as I know that today prepares tomorrow
I

I ask
16 years of my yesterday did not prepare me
as I straddled life and death
as many who were fine and ripe
who were my friends
fell
when we together eyed as we paced time
holding fire in our hands
and in our hearts, cherishing simple things of life,
which we sought
and fought for
and pleaded with our country about —
they are not here now, the fine men and women
they crushed on the earth, as if they were over-ripe fruit
   and burst
now, I ponder about them
for
I
shared song
and moments which made life magic with them
as I eye some of my countrymen
with dappled eyes and vague looks
and at times with hostility
I think of them in drifting thought
with questions whose answers are deadend streets,
and others
their soft convictions, remain hard unclosed eyes
I miss them
for how we shared life
and how they fell out of it
for
they are not here now
with their laughter
with their frowns
with their fears and smells
which made *them* them
my simple friends
they are not here, only in memory;

I meet their lovers
or children who remind me of them
and that
in this time where fine boys and girls come and go like that
the moment is dazzling and dangerous
ah
in the heart of this time
it is simple things which are forgotten
desecrated
and defiled
they are fossilised into a past which is out of reach
it is in memory that these moments
crimson
they dazzle
they buzz like very long moments of a terribly long day,
which will not pass.

In Stockholm they say the winter is too long
the summer too short
and since the hour of spring is dazzling,
they celebrate and share it
they do it every year
in drink and song
in England they can be aloof
some shrewd
but all love the Queen, she is magic to them all
even as the Eastern bloc crumbled
soon
all of us will come to know the finesse of the moment,
when a thought cherished and shared
can
because it has hope of simple men and women
warm snow
ah
where
where are those moments which can be magic
and dazzling

and can bind us together
us
the human race
who built bridges and tunnels
who reach the sky
who reach the fathom of the sea
we
the human race.
Where
where is that moment
which can startle us to life!
to love life
so we can dare death
and even as we die
we can say
we tried the best to its limits.

Where
where is that magic moment!
to drop from our minds and hearts
to ripple and form
binding us
growing and flowing and growing
binding us in its spread and flow
tying us
in time, in space, in life
making us
our brief life
a glitter and sparkle of ripples of hope!
there are men
and there are women
they walk with straight shoulders
they walk with tall gaits
and heads thrown back as if they were antennae
and unblinking eyes and propped ears
they listen with the style and grace of animals
whose every fibre is a nerve
saying

life —
life is worth living,
can be lived and must be lived
in their grace
in their search of life
in their search of those simple things which make it life
which make it be lived
which make it be sought after
which now and then startle with its essence
its joy
its sparkle and glitter in the eye of a beautiful woman
or the embrace of a man who loves life
or the man, or the woman
whose smile
whose eye
when they throw their arms open in their laughter which
   can ring and
ripple
with their shoulders
wide and deep like an open door
can make us say
if life is so simple
why can't it be lived
if it is so brief
why can't we let it be lived
in its brevity
in its simplicity
in its joy
why can't we let it be lived
in its brief magic
ah my friends
in far-flung places of the world
caught in floods and cyclones
in Latin America
in Mozambique
in Bangladesh
the Kurds
the Palestinians

the Red Indian
the child
in the deep of the Transkeian rural area
in the dangerous street of New York and Soweto
where
every second, every hour
as if life is a disease
it is sought with the best of cunning
hunted
snared
to be cornered and clubbed and clubbed and clubbed
even when it huddles
startled by cruelty and hatred against it
it knows
for it has heard and it has seen
how
if life is snared and cornered
on TV
newspaper
and radio
there is no mercy!
my friends
in this heart of this time
it is simple things which are forgotten
desecrated
and defiled
they are fossilised into a past which is out of reach
the night
and the gloomy sky
are deep and fathomless
they conspire in silence
they are witness and merciless
they make us say
we are here
for what
is it at the wrong place, the wrong time, with wrong
   words,
really?

yes
if the bright day is unbearable
and the twilight sleepless
and if the bright moon finds us hungry
how can the night
or a thoughtful weather be livable?
ah
what have we done with life
to make it so frighteningly unlivable
I
I ask
the good men and women
the fine boys and girls
those of my hour and time
can we transform the word stop!
can we make it an act
I
I ask
for I love life
I ask
let's dare to be different
in this time
here where life has become a dangerous species
made so
by plenty and wretched poverty
let the wretched of our time
the men
children
the women
who witness the sun rise and the sun set
the moon climb and the moon fall
the star twinkle and fade
every day every hour bewildered by life
let them see in our eye
our dare for the mighty
let our eye in its unshakable belief teach them to catch
  a fish
and to refuse to be given it

let them see in our gait
which is shaped by our love for life
the defiance and hatred
of the wealthy
who abscess this earth
with ghettoes and shanty towns
with prejudice
and bombs and guns
let them read in our face
and pick from our world
hope,
let them, as the child does,
crawl
stand
hold onto human civilization:
the wealth of the human race
of the time and space lived by generations of man
let them utter their first word —
no!
let the multitudes from the shanties
of time
of history
of culture
hold onto the helm and horizon of time
and in the loudest voice
which will blow the TV, newspapers and radio
blow them to utter silence
let the multitudes of this time
say
stop!
how will that word sound
how will it strike the heart
how will it embrace time
if in one voice
after they crawl
after they hold and stand up
after they take the first step, taking us into a new time
how

how will they stop
so this time can stop
how
how will they take the step as they make us take it
that first step into the next time
how will it be like
what will they say
which language will they use
to say no stop!
to this time
to where we are
from Africa and Asia
North and South America
from Europe
if the many
who live in holes
who eat shit
who thirst
if they say no, stop!
if they crawl like a baby does, out of their holes
if they stand up from the cold pavement
if they stop looking at us from below, from the bottom
their eyes cast at us as if to heaven
for mercy
for a penny
for perhaps a slight streak of guilt in us
for pity
if they crawled out
if they stood up
if they took the first step
to take us with them into the new time
how
how would it feel
what would happen?
here
I talk about the multitudes
whose minds have been shattered by daily hunger
or their children —

I talk here about those who know that thirst
like a blow
can blow lights out of eyes
I talk here about the hundreds who know
that the cold wind can turn flesh into steel
I
I talk about these multitudes
who know that
in the heart of this time
it is simple things which have been forgotten
desecrated
and defiled
they are fossilised into a past which is out of reach
they know
as they watch the rich and the mighty
that they and them
have lost the magic of simple things
to share
to share a song
to share a magic moment
even time which is witness and silent
shakes its head in disbelief
ah
where
where is the human race?
I ask
from a glitter of light and the green leaf
which dance and dance with each other
in the broad daylight
I ask
from the gloomy sky which seems to look askance
at glass and the height of skyscrapers
I ask
from the clouds which hang softly
below an aeroplane
I ask
from the yellow dazzle of rows upon rows of sunflowers
hanging their heads in buzzing yellow when the sun sets

I ask
and I ask
I ask the eyes of a lover
I ask the green in the open field
which jumps and throws its hands into the air
as it rides the mountain, the ravine and the slope
where
where is the human race?
to give life a touch of eternity
here
I do not ask anyone to fear death or to cling to life
here
I ask for our want to make life magic,
since it is so brief
since it is so loved
since it is so unquestionably rare
can't it be shared
why
why do we visit life as if it were a cemetery?
why
why do we take to it nostalgia and sorrow
or despair
I ask here
for on subways in cities I've been to
on stations
and in buses which we ride on endless journeys
the youth, as if a dying rose
hang their eye
and the old dare not look at them
as they shake and muzzle their life
as if a puppy tearing a piece of rag
as they smash their skull against glass
I ask
for in the sexless gait of a young woman it is graffiti on
   the wall
proclaiming a cynical time to come
I say so
for when young boys speak

17

and say what they have seen
and hear voices of old and dying men
it is when time is elegant in being senseless
ah
let those whose arms are stretched out
whose shoulders are as broad as an open door
let them embrace this moment
let them hold it with soft fingers and weigh it on their
    strong arms
let their legs which with stealth
have run
reared
and walked on the horizon of this time
tell us
let them tell us
what they have heard and seen and touched
so we can share their eye
which tells us, we are on the move again
to search
to find
a place, a time when, when the hurt children
those that live where once I lived
where the streets are wet
are muddy
are dangerous
and know blood
the streets
which have left itching sores on their legs
on their hands
on their body — sores, the plague of the poor,
the children
with no trees to make a shadow for them
with no shade where they can play
they are children
though they are black though it doesn't matter if they die
they are children
I come from there, once I was a child there
where cars, blind in their speed, fly past

where corpses in streets are commonplace
where no one explains the articulate vulgarity
and eloquence of lifelessness
where every day children long to hear someone say:
I'm not far away from you, don't fear
but everything is in the distant
at the tip of the hip, life is cheap
it is not life which made it so
you can ask all those men and women
who have fought
who fell
who are in cages or are hunted
they are witness
the night
and the twilight
and the broad daylight is witness too
they ask
as we talk at each other at the top of the voice
as we make sounds whose light blinds the eye
as the tips of our fingers, from which we hang,
begin to bleed
as the mind throbs and pounds in delirium
in Asia
Latin America and Africa
where the soil and the landscape look like a cement slab
where huts scatter
like the remaining limbs of a body plagued with leprosy
and rain water takes the soil and huts away
where the sun, merciless
beats and pounds the centre of the head
here
at the backyard of time
where people wait and wait and wait
and time
like pain, will not go away
multitudes stare with eyes as many as stars
they are dead silent
in 1991

when the 21st century is here
they know
there are those who speak, see, hear and touch for them
as they wait
and time, like pain will come, will not pass
I say
it is not life which put them there
it is not time which put them there
nor is it anything else which put those
whose time flies with their life like a sputnik
and work, and poverty and programs
eat their life as cancer would a cell
in ghettoes
in shanty towns
in factories
in mines
in farm lands
in hard streets, and wars they never planned or intended
where buses and trains and trucks carry them
to and fro, fro and to
every day every night
life bashing —
where ailments hatch and creep like mushrooms to the
 surface
here the silence is tangible
it has stealth and skill
it snares
it awaits all of us
this silence
which looks like a motionless tree
which feels like an insect walking in parts of the body
 you cannot reach
it is alive
the silence in its utter silence
awaits us
asks us:
if we have ears to hear what do we say
or eyes which see: what can we do

for
this world, which we share and shape
whose corners you can touch if you stretch your arms
whose roof you can reach if you stand up
was and is ours
we make and have made it
because
all of us die from what we all have eaten and have done
so it is
the story of the silent village
and the silent township
and suburb
and town
the silence, as lovers know
is no good
lovers know
that when at the end of time eyes have been scratched
and noses and cheeks punched and slapped
when helpless they stare at each other in silence
which holds the hurt
the heart breaks, time stops
and the darkness holds to the eye
planting as if a spear piercing the flesh
despair in the body
nothing can be saved
but what is it which makes us do this
do animals do it
do the stars
or the sun or does the moon
do the rivers
what is it that makes us walk
talk
embrace
and be left with despair
not knowing how to look into each other's eye
what is it
can the good men and the good women tell me
can they

21

in their wisdom
say something —
what is it?
what would we hear if the multitude spoke?
if they broke their silence
what is it we would hear
would we hear it?
if they left their drums
and their song
if they said they can now catch a fish
what is it that we would hear
if the TV and the radio and the newspaper
were to be filled with their voice
would we remain literate?
I ask
for me, I said I can read, I can write
I ask
for I said we can see
we feel
I ask
the good men and women of this time
would we
would we hear and see
would we hear and see and remain literate?
I
I ask
since in the twilight of my likes
when we held the hot alarm clock with bare hands,
bare faced
time
like a mother, with great care, hands the baby to its
  father
or
a father, with great care, shows a baby its mother
it brought us eyeball to eyeball with truth
that
when the bottom gets hot, the top begins to boil
we learnt

in the heat and chill of time
that in any heart a glow flickers
it can die out
it can burn and burn and burn
it is love for life
in each heart, in every heart like a song
whose words inform and are informed by life
the flicker burns and burns and dances
gnawing, seeking out, seeking life
we learnt
the envy
the uncertainty
the lesson of the flickering of the multitudes
in fear
at times in a raw love for life
they hesitate
they ask
they hold on to silence with their life
becoming as dangerous as a sharp stone
and their eye and their brave expressions betray nothing
as they betray us for a cup of coffee
so it is
this time we learnt
as their men hid axes to chop our heads
and their women
as if their loins were fathomless holes
in betrayal
they swallowed us
as we wondered whether the next moment
would shut out our eyes forever
it is like that
if we do not understand or know or learn
that we are not the pace of anything else
but life
how can we live it
or let it be lived
I
I ask

23

for this time
these moments and space are dangerous
like the mad flood
or lifeless cyclone which speeds like an insane train
or aeroplane which loses its nerve in the sky
packed with people
and dives and plunges down
my friend
it is very dangerous here
I lack the words to say it as it is
for
you only have to go to there
Africa
Asia
and Latin America
you only have to go to the villages, the ghettoes and the shanty towns
to listen to the ghost voice
of the granite and stubborn stone of the mountain
the voice of the rail track and road
of the wild bush
of the wind and heat of the sun
to hear how they gnawed life
how they nibbled youth and middle age
lungs and lust
fingers and feet of those who dwell here
those
in ghettoes and shanty towns
who built this time, this life and the civilization
with bare life.

Ask if you can
the lungs and heart
the lives of the multitudes, how time tamed their youth
how rocks snatched their lust and kidneys
how rock desert bush and endless empty space
in eloquence, like a gas chamber
sucked, swallowed and dried life

lives
so: rivers and roads
rail tracks and space can grow and grow
making time a space which can be reached
which can become rungs of life
which we live and lead
using burning lust burnt and lost in rock
in the desert
in the wind
using despair, which with the spirit of ghosts
still sings on rows and rows of telephone wires
where birds sing in chorus with the bundles of resting
   souls
with heaps of life lost
in the insatiable fathom of civilisation
for what
Africa
Asia
Latin America, for what?
I ask
me the son of this time
I ask for what
why did the skyscrapers throw life from heights so high
why did the mines swallow and finish life
as if it were gasoline
why did the untamed rivers, as if they were sewage,
gaggle and choke with life
of those from the village and the ghettoes and the shanty
   town
for what
why
we, we have forgotten the simple things
those which we can share
we, we have fossilised into a past which is unreachable
little things which make life life
like a kiss, a hug
a hand-hold
which come from large hearts of men and women

who can share.

Ah
let the men and women of this earth
of this time
of this knowledge made with ash to ash
soil to soil
claim the past for the future
for the present
as one little man said
the present is dangerous, and blood-stained
in my country mad and insane men hold our necks
hold guns to our foreheads
they play Russian roulette with the nation
these men and women are white
who made these men and women and why?
men wipe their whiskers women wag their tails
because they think we are their creation
but even what they have made
they would not treat with such meanness
to create a ghetto
to create a place without a toilet
to create a place without streets and gates
to create houses created for crowding people
to create a place without water for people
to create hunting grounds
to create laws for hunting grounds
to create laws and hunting grounds for people
to herd them
to herd and pen people and mock them
to mock them and to use them
to use them
like a pick
like pliers
like a hammer
to use penned, horded people
people who live on hunting grounds
to use them

like a rock
like a pole
to make them poor
to make poor people in hunting grounds
hunting grounds with hunting laws for poor people
it is here
where the white people
among the black people
where they created hunting grounds
they created spies
the spies tell on poor people
the spies tell on poor black people
the spies tell on poor black people to white people
some black people join white people
the spies tell white people
so and so is pissing
so and so is shitting
so and so is sleeping with so and so
so and so didn't shit or piss today
so and so says the hunting grounds are quiet
so and so says there's noise in the hunting grounds
there's white people in the hunting grounds who smile
they hug
they kiss
they sleep
they join in the noise of the hunting ground
the spies tell other white people about white people
the spies tell on those poor people
in my country mad and insane men hold our necks
they hold guns to our foreheads
they play Russian roulette with the nation
these men and women are black and white
these men
these women
these blacks and whites
these people
have left droplets of blood on my shoes
these droplets don't ever dry up

in a plane
on a train
in a bus
in different cities
I see the droplets on my shoes
me
I will not hide them
I walk I fly I ride I cycle
in big and small cities
me
I can't forget
I don't understand
the droplets are still fresh and wet
on my shoes
they shine like a mirror
they buzz like bees
these droplets on my shoes
I keep looking at them
I keep looking at them and at the men and women
black and white women
speechless
I
I hope they too can see them
I see these droplets even when it is dark
dark
dark as hell
in the dark I hear voices
in the dark I hear laughter
when it is not broad daylight
voices and laughter, whispers and murmurs
dance and jive
sing and sigh
the voices are very busy buzzing
about fine men and women
about the droplets on my shoes
in the dark
in the hunting grounds
there is noise

the spies know
there is noise here
in the shanty in the squatter camp, in the village
there is noise here
it whispers
it whistles like the song of telephone wires
it keeps us all awake
the white men
the white women
the black and white
the spies are restless
I walk
I stop
I run
I walk
in the hunting grounds
in the heart of this time
it is simple things which are forgotten
desecrated
and defiled
what is it that we need
a thought to share
about the bread we broke and together ate
a song we shared, which left magic in our hearts

In this time
in this world of black and white
of men and women
of squint-eyed black and white
black and white men and women
who mismatch shoes to look like bananas on their feet
me
I think
what kind of men and women are these
who can't even wear shoes properly
they are mad
they are insane
they spy

they are in a hurry
they have no time
they are running to the office
to read reports of spies
they read reports to prepare for a carnage
ah
they broke the Eastern bloc
while the men there read reports
they read reports
they find out that there was no bread to break
in the Eastern bloc
and in the Third World
they read reports in their offices
they prepare armies
when they came to know there was no bread
there was no place to sleep
they read it in a report of a spy
they prepared guns and bombs and armies
they packaged a carnage in a hurry
they forgot to wear shoes properly
they were in a hurry
to the office
to make a phone call
to prepare to plan armies
to prepare to plan bombs and guns
to hand out guns
these people have no fun
they are serious people
they heard about the noise
they read about it from a report
they read the report of a spy
the spy said
the spy said
the spy said
the spy said
the spy said (is it true?)
it takes long to answer that question
the spy said

the spy said
the spy said
the noise is growing in the dungeons
the spy said prepare the bombs and guns
prepare the army
the hordes don't want to be picks or poles or spades
prepare the armies
the noise is restless the restlessness is the noise
prepare
prepare the armies
the noise sings like rows and rows of telephone wires
the spy said
the voices are like millions of footsteps
prepare
quickly
prepare

Me
I want to show the spy my shoes
I want to show the spy the freshness and wetness on my
    shoes
we worked hard last night
in the dark
as the army worked
after it, we carried people
we carted people into cars and carried some
after the blades and the spears and the axes
after the guns
after the boots
after the noise died down
I saw droplets on my shoes
ah my friends
sometimes I wonder
when's the express coming
with its speedy wind it must come
at night
in the morning
it must come

the Third World Express must come
at dawn
in the twilight
like the wind
like a river
like a mad dam.

What is it we need
a thought to share
a song
what is it we want?
if we have eyes to see
and ears to hear
if we can touch
if we can see, hear and touch
what is it that we need
a song
a thought
bread
what is it that we need
in the twilight of life
in the noise
in its song
for it is in earnest and honesty I ask
Africa
Asia
Latin America
how
how is life lost
when it is lived in pits
in cities of the world
in the heart of this time
where young men
where young women
in delirium
in insanity
whirl and whirl and whirl
seeing the world turn and turn around

up
and down and upside down
where the old wait
wait alone
and die alone leaving a stench in our memory.

In my country
the young have fought oh Africa
they fought
they fell
they were fine men and women
I
I recall some of them
now gone
for what
Africa tell me for what?
me I hope
I hope I never forget to tell them
that they are not the lost generation
I hope
I hope I remember to tell them
if they lived again
they must like they did
with the voice of the hoot of the train
with the loudness of the glow of a full moon
with the whistle of a twinkling star
with the cry of a speeding car
they must say
they are not pliers
they are not spades or poles or picks
they must say
they are not rock or bar
they must
like the noise they came from
want
rear and roll
roar
wait and roll

climb and ebb
flow and wait
rear and roll
roar
in the thick and the thin
in the distance
in the inside
in the noise and whisper
in the murmur
in the destiny
in the blend and buzz and glitter
in the breaking of noise and colour
Africa
Asia
Latin America and ghettoes of mighty cities
in the eye of a goat
in the grace of an eating cow
in the embrace of a stretching landscape
they must say
in the breath of the sky
and the roll and flow of the wind
in the speed of a train
in the height of a plane
in Africa
Asia
in South Africa
the noise starts and stops
it is a murmur
of the young and fresh and fine
it is the whisper
it is the whistle of the collapsing Eastern bloc
it is a rumble of seventy years of betrayal
it is a murmur
it is a whisper
it is a noise
it is hope
patched
on rows upon rows of telephone wires

it is that wind
it is that voice buzzing
it is whispering and whistling on the wires
miles upon miles upon miles
on the wires in the wind
in the subway track
in the rolling road
in the not silent bush
it is the voice of the noise
here it comes
the Third World Express
they must say, here we go again.

MONGANE WALLY SEROTE

Come and Hope With Me

FOR O.R. AND CASSIUS MAKE ("THE PILOT")
WHO TAUGHT ME ABOUT WAR AND PEACE

In that day and in that life
we lived in dreams and also in desire
we hoped and believed
even when the day crushed and popped our time
turning the sky crimson and the night cast upon us
dark and cold shadows
and the sky, stern, hovered above us
we lived in dreams and hopes

strong
we sang
we chanted
we jumped and danced
and we were aware of the steep and slope of the road
and of the load on our shoulders.
with skill
we lived in dreams and desire
loving life with our large hearts
even though nostalgia like fire
burnt and burnt our gut

all these
we mounted, jumped and chanted
our eyes fixed on the road

remember
the passion of our hearts
the blinding ache and pain
when we heard the hysterical sobs
of our little children crying against fate
which violated them and offered them no life
or the frightening cry of a man
who climbs life with no hope in his heart
we heard these. we knew them. we absorbed them
but we surged forward
knowing that life is a promise and that that promise is us
the promise lives in the staring eye of a song
it is

let me quickly say
those of us
with timid hearts
and large fears and insatiable greed
and women who no longer could nurture life
who betrayed us
they fell
they shrivelled
they rotted
they left a stench in our lives
and they went their way
away into the distance which makes the future
and the present
and the past – dangerous to live in

we
we eyed each other
even as the pounding of the heart felt like thunder
we climbed the steep path up
even when the horizon was shut
we faced it, approached it
went to it even as it receded like a mirage
we will come upon it one of these days
in the full moon of our night
which huddles the melancholy of our hopes
nurturing vitriol which we must overcome
and this night and this light we must make
to reveal strength inside us
in the inner insides of our heart and gut
of the township
where men huddle in the shadows of alleys to urinate
and women squat with starry eyes behind shacks
and relieve themselves, listening to voices of drunken men
we came to know then
that when nature calls, no horizon will remain shut

so
in the day

and in the night
against the steep and slope of the road
we arrive here
when the white people did not expect us
we arrive now
we ask
even when the blacks who betrayed us
expect us
they did not expect us
the horizon is wide and round and blind
and that is our path which is everywhere
we arrive
it is only fate
and it is only hunger
which lards us with blows and sends us helter-skelter
ah
now that you know why some of us are not here
and you know
that their tale hangs in the air at finger tip
waiting to be told that it sails in the air
and is threaded in the curling cloud
and that it glitters in the raindrop
and that on the soil their souls lie silent and patient
full of hope that
a dream of people is not a bubble and will not burst

so
here we are then
stuck
holding on to the memory and the story
holding on to the child's fate
and cry
and
like time, life goes on
ticks
finds some space every and anywhere
our life holds on to a dream
a desire

that in the weight of despair
the imperishable particle of hope
remains for life to be lived in its brevity
that
as the raging fire ate the bare hand of generations
may the strength of that pain be the hope of its children
to be in harmony
with the protea flower
the purple jacaranda
and the lush yellow and green of the sunflower which
    strikes
the light in the sky
and climbs and jumps, stands and dances
holds
and sings in the wind
chants and throws its arms into the horizon
like ringing laughter holds the setting Magaliesberg sun
this light
cuddles the ripe yellow mango
and the green avocado pear
and the rows upon rows of green and yellow orange trees
guava trees
and banana trees
and the ripe provocative pawpaws
in the lush land of Tzaneen
and the whistling and flowing brittle juice of the vine
in the sprawling green of Stellenbosch
and the sticky heat of Natal
where the wind and the sea and the mirage
caress and sweat
sing and embrace life like lovers
and the smell of the sea and fish
in harsh and mysterious ways
remind one
that here Africa ends
in gliding and flowing waves towards Cape Point
that there Africa takes breath
sighs

at the end of the earth
where the mountains and the sky
stare
the sea
and the fish smell and the heat
and the drizzling rain
and the rolling hillocks and mountains
and the silent scream of beauty frolic
saying beauty is beauty when it is beauty
is fathomless
and laughs and giggles
and is untouchable but holds you
and asks –
what is life that it has to be lived
is beauty not the autarchy in life?
like time
it ticks and ticks
like life
it lives and heaves embracing the shut horizon
and the open sky
lives in the whistle of the open sea waves
and in the colours of the bloomed Namaqualand flowers
which watch the hard boulder embedded and scattered
lying and spread in the land
the flower colours burst
melt and flow
dapple
and scream
crawl and climb and blind the blue sky
with a soft voice
the colours here
whisper and whistle
dance and are still in the air
they watch the wind blow and kiss the light of day.

here
desire cries and cracks like a whip
even for the children to know

that
it is here where life plants its sustenance in our hearts
it is here where the tumult of life begins
it howls and calls
cracks and pounds
saying we must return

we must return to the crying eye
the broken face and the devastated gait
the sagging shoulder
which tell us that here the feather of life has been broken
we must return
to the boy and the girl the man and the woman
whose beauty is the suspicion that life can be lived
and they hold on to it
so, in the dusk of their lives
how can anyone call for civil war?

our land needs peace
its soil is heavy and sags with blood
we do not want civil war
we need the simple things of life
to drink and eat
and to know
we must return

we must return to the simple questions which hang large
in the eyes and the faces
in the gait
in the sagging shoulders and dangling body
in the broken brittle egg of life
of a man
of a boy
of a woman
of a child
whose guitar whose song rings at the edge of the horizon
is wafted through the blades of the sunlight
pops and breaks with grief and hysterical laughter

in the blue sky we see hovering above us
in the clear air we breathe
in the goodwill of our heart as we walk the dangerous
   street
we must return

ah
let us return
to the man
the girl
to the boy
the woman
whose beauty is the suspicion that life can be lived
as with their whispering footsteps
in the alley of the dark
and near the rubbish bin where flies hover and buzz
they return once more and over again
they ask the fly
they ask our blind passing footsteps
they ask the heat and the cold
they ask the day and the night
they ask
with intimate secrets and hope not to fear
they ask
with fear not to hope
that that life which must be lived can be lived
they and us
we do not need a civil war
we must return
to fetch the squatterman and the squatterchild
the squatterwoman
and the squatterlife where traitors are bought and made
where killers
carrying spears and sticks and axes and guns
and with blood in the eye
they watch the rich
and watch the whites
watch the poor

they watch themselves
they watch themselves watch and wait

we do not want a civil war

ah
i call the preacherman
the medicineman and woman
the bones
the indunaman and the baas
i call the traindriver and taxidriver
who have seen life speed on their wheels to death
i call the chief
i call the traditionalman and woman
i call witchcraft and the boere
i go to the kgotla
i go to the marketwoman and the carver of art
to the singer

let us return to life
though it is made so cheap in our dwellings
because we hire us to kill us
we must i say, return
if prayer or science or spirit will return us here
it does not matter how
we must
live here, where we were born
there's nothing we can do nor anywhere else we can go
we live here
we live life here
we dream
desire and hope here
it is here where those we maimed live
here
where the graves of those we killed are
here
where the eyes startled by our speech stare
let us return and surge

it is here where our own graves must be
and our children whom we give life and must give
   dreams
will live here
we do not want any civil war
we must return to life and live it here
where we must overcome racism and tribalism
and know, being black and white men and women
Jew and umZulu
English and moTswana and Indian
umXhoza
under this sun
we must return to the labourer and the youth
the farmhand and the domestic servant
to the intellectual
it is to them that civil war will happen
we must return and ask
civil war against whom by whom?

we must return
to the song of the sugarcane cutter
to the gumboot dance of the mineworker
to the song of the street digger and migrant labourer
we must return to the businessman
and the hostel dweller and we must say life must be lived
we cannot and shall not return later
later will be too late
we must return now
we want to drink eat and know
we want to return to life
in the land of our birth
the land of the mango and the pineapple
in the land of the banana
of the red and white grape we want to return
to this land of large and chains of mountains
this land of hillocks
in this land of the sea and the fish and the shark
in the land of the mielie stock the diamond and the gold

we want to return to the cheetah with its stare for life
and the monkey with its thoughtful pose and dexterity
the baboon
the giraffe with its grace and sight into the distance
to the speed of the gazelle and its shrewd innocence
and to the ugliness of the beauty of the crocodile
to the strength of the elephant and buffalo
and to the spirit of no surrender of the hyena
we must return to the lush lust of our life
living in the song
in the sound
the rhythm and dance of the drum and the violin
the trumpet and the piano
we must return
to the music of our life
we must say this is who we are in life
and in death
when we have lived in the full heart of a dream
and the desire
it is we who must have lived the conflict of life
and in the last days of our life
when we hand over time to the young and pass
let them remember us with the glitter of our eye
which says hope is hope when it speaks in silence

ah
we must return to the dream and the desire
we must go back
to know
believing in the wisdom of time and generations
this wisdom
which like a large rough rock
rolls and rolled
floats and is bashed against bank and time
is washed by the river. is struck by heat.
is caressed by wind in the roll and ebb
in the heat and cold of time and river
is shaped and smoothed

and stands with time to say here we are

here we are
of time and of generations which flowed in the banks
and the heat and cold
we have rolled and still roll
shaped by time and we shape it
we shine the spear against the full moon
and the shining sun
to shield peace in the time of our life
we spent the wisdon of time and generations
in the depth of our death life must be found

a seed
for life and of life must be found
we do not want a civil war
who are they who now call for civil war
when
in the heart of this nation there is deep desire for peace

they fear and are greedy
and so
they call for our blood and limb and life of generations
who are they
because of avarice and personal power
they call for civil war. against whom? by whom?
come
amaZulu
amaXhoza
Jew
baSotho
maNdebele come answer me
maVenda maSwati
civil war against whom by whom for whom
baTswana maShangana
Boers maPedi
the English
the teacher the worker

the woman and the man
the child
the nurse and the businessman
we do not want any civil war
we do not want any racial or tribal war
we do not want the spilling of blood
we have known no peace
we want the simple things of life
to drink
to eat
to know
to sing and to dance
we want to return to dreams
to desire
to hope
we want to work and to build
we want to walk and to talk
we must return to the will and wish to live

we must return
to the lush flesh of the mango
the peach
the vine and the sunflower
the sea
and to the rough and tough mountains of the Transvaal
to its west and the Orange Free State
to Namaqualand
we must glide in the swiftness of the cheetah
and the speed of the gazelle
we must delight in the orchestra of our many languages
in the land of our birth of many colours
which strike the sun and say is this not beauty?

we must return
to dreams of dreams
to the break of dawn and its shimmering sounds
of the cock and the hyena and the lion and the elephant
when they scream to the joy of a new day

with its splashed colours of red and yellow and mauve
and silver horizon
we must return to hope and dream
to life and peace
we must return to the tall serene of the giraffe
we must return to carry peace with the strength of a
   buffalo
the lion and the rhino
the cheetah and elephant
and glide with it on our shoulders and legs
we must carry it
for peace like freedom is heavy

here
we want peace
there has been carnage here
the air smells of blood and the stench of lost life
like a mirage hangs in the wind
the souls of those who never lived life
cries in the air
their eyes stare at us in want and disbelief
and their footsteps echo in time
here
the gunshot
the grenade
fire
they rage and rage pounding life down
the blacks are dying
the whites are rich and fearful
here
there is no peace

we must return
like rain
after a drought
like the smell of the soil after rain
we must return like summer after winter
no

we do not want any civil war
we will not become bereft of vision
that hope
that courage
that passion
that desire must reside in wisdom
we cherish that noble thought of civilisation
that life must be lived in full
we must now seek this

we must return
to the rainbow of our land
this nation of shimmering colours and shades
let's glide and stride and straddle
like a rainbow across the sky
look and watch
like the rainbow after the rain
in the sky
in the sun
sing and ring
call
hail and chime
like the shimmering rainbow in the wind
let's whisper and whistle
let's ululate
call on peace to come to our land in our life
we must
like the ant return to work
we must like game migrate back to life
in multitudes we must now return
we do not want any civil war

Angola and Mozambique
Somalia
who is it who wasted your limb and life and time
we must oh Africa return
to life to work to knowledge
let us return

we lived in dreams and desire
we lived in hope
even when our day crushed and popped
turning the sky crimson
and the night cast upon us cold shadows of dark skies
we did live in dreams and hopes
we loved life
we chose beauty and fought the beast
in the liquid of our blood and in the depth of our heart
eyeball to eyeball with life
we lived in dreams
also in desire
and we hoped and believed
we sang
we chanted
we jumped and danced
loving life with large hearts
it is the giant heart of the generations which bears
holds
hopes that the wisdom of the old remains when the old
  pass
the growth of the new is fragile in our hands
it is inside care where a fight is taut
and care is a cushion where life rests

we must return
to the African heart
to the spirit whose dignity stood the pain of humiliation
of poverty
when our children played with mud dolls
and came to spit in our faces
and invented the necklace
and stunned us with burning people alive
clubbing them in the view of the whole world to see
when with anger they took to the streets
with impunity
they bought life with death
as they rendered life more cheap than dirty water

it was in the township and in the village
from where the smell of burning flesh came
we could then have sung
flesh is burning
flesh is burning
flesh is burning

but we buried the dead
we nurtured the maimed
we promised freedom to the dead and the maimed
we asked for sacrifice
from the women
the men and the children we called on them
since time was witness but accomplice
since history was so merciless and cruel
even as it repeated itself
in devastating life
in burning flesh
in maiming and emerging bloody with carnage
in rolling and rolling death and the dead
we said
in life
in time
in history the cycle cycles and returns
to cycle again
to claim that life must be lived in change
to say
we must return to dream
to desire
we must return

we must return
like the sun and the moon
like the seasons
we must return

but since we are human
we must return to claim change

with its quality to change things
we must return
we must return to make things better
with science
with prayer
with witchcraft with whatever
the human race must return
since this is the call of the human race
we must return
to claim change and change change to change for the better
we must return

we must return
to examine
to look and seek and to search
in the ritual of marriage and child birth
in the death and witchcraft and the church
in the taking off of the clothes
which the poor and the Christians
believe and die by
which they get poorer and illiterate
and locked out of the world
as they sing and chant with hysteria
as blindness and deafness and muteness hold them
and embrace them
we must return to know
it is these at times which abort our freedom
which shackle us
which bind us
which lock us
and hold us and rivet us to bondage and ignorance
these rituals
let us return to look and search and seek an out
into the light of the moon and the sun
into the light of the world which we so painfully built
ah
let us seek an out

into education and the open world
and bring to it from our shacks and shanties
where non-racialism resides
from where we are tired of senseless death
and cheap life
let us bring to it the story of how we negotiated
how we gave and took
how with large hearts and large minds
we hung with our life on patience
and suspense
and we gave
and we waited
and we said this is a country for all of us
even the killers and the torturers
the blacks and the whites if ever there was such
it is our land
even for those we killed and those who cry forever
this is our land

we do not want any civil war or any war
we have fought and died and lived and wandered
the past must not come into this time
i ask let us now pause
what do we want
what do we need
where are we going
let us pause and let us return
what are we supposed to be doing here on earth
let us pause
we have been thrashed and pounded
we have been between the anvil and the heat
but we have now with great pain and red blood
we have i say
the child

it must not die in our hands
i ask
may the child know

and sing
and dream
and grow and walk and talk like a bird
there
the child

ah
i will return
like the cycle
like the sun
like the moon
like the day and the night and the seasons
to say
my child this place and this earth
spins and spins and spins
my child
here we dream and desire
we hope
child
the seed of this hope is buried deep
it lies in the eye and ear
in the sullen and silent face
it lies deep in time
it awaits you
with large and fat and tall stories
it awaits you
to climb the steep and slope
this hope awaits you to hope
come and hope with me
when it is dark
when it rains
when it is cold here
when the scream shatters the heart
when there is nothing to do but huddle
come
come and hope with me child

come I ask you and hope with me

for on that day
in April
they nearly crushed my hope
when we stood under the broad daylight and vast sky
and we stood unable to weep
when even the wind which breezed in the heat of the day
could not shake one leaf
and the shadows of trees weighed heavily on our life
in that April day and heat
i asked
why must i hope and love
why
for i know i do not know how many have been killed
in the bush
in the streets
in prison
i do not know how many have been burnt
melted in acid to powder
i do not know how many have been killed
and disposed of as if they were dirty paper
and were buried
they disappeared from life and the day forever
into the dark of the night and time

on that April day
under the broad daylight and sky
when the day crushed and popped our time
turning the sky crimson and the night cast upon us
dark and cold shadows
and the sky, stern, hovered upon us
when they shattered our hope
and like a crashing cup in a quiet house
the news reached us

soon
we stood
at the pool of blood and the motionless body
on the driveway in broad daylight

in Dawn Park
Chris Hani
like a broken cup lay
they shot him in the head and chest
he lay still holding his car keys in one hand
and clutching newspapers under his armpit
he lay awkwardly on his belly
in his tracksuit and running shoes next to his car
on a broad daylight
they hurt us
we huddled and stood still like leaves unaware of the
    breeze
we stood still

and time said nothing
they shot and killed him
they want a boerestaat and racism and civil war
they want Zulu tribalism
they killed him because there was too much progress
for peace.

we buried Chris
we sang
we chanted
we jumped and danced
we had become aware of the steep and slope of the road
and the load on our shoulders

with skill
we seized on dreams

here we must hope and dream
we must

we must dream and desire and hope
we must fight and hope
we must hope and fight

here we must hope and fight
we must

child
come and hope and dream with me
come

come
i need you when i dream
when i hope
when i fight
come, i need you

we must you and i
when history repeats itself
we must return
to dream and hope and fight
for the best for all of us
that is why we are here
come and hope with me oh child
come

the driveways are bloody
was it at night or in the morning
in the Harare dusk or dawn
when they trapped Joe Gqabi in the driveway
and pinned him down like a cornered animal
shot him and killed him
he fell splashing the driveway with his blood

come oh friend
i need you when i dream and when i fight
i need you when i hope
when i am huddled
and it rains and it is cold
i need you when like an elephant protecting its little ones
i come to fight for peace

we must you and i when history repeats itself
we must return
to dream
to hope
to fight
for the beauty of human life is that we came here to think
and to plan
and to see the future
and to know and to drink and to eat and to have a home

i say
come
come and hope and be with me
when they plan a carnage
when they clean their rifles
when in the early hours of the morning
and in the night
they come dragging history in red blood
come and be with me
come and hope and dream with me

come
when it is lonely
when they have frightened me
when with their noises and footsteps
with their trucks and horses
when they have come for you and for me
and the stars are witness
and the moon is witness
and the sun is witness
when history repeats itself

come
come and be with me
come and hope and dream with me
come my friend and be with me
come let's repeat history together
in prison

in the trenches
in the face of the might of death
come
and sing
and dance
and jump
and chant with me

come
we must hope and dream and desire
we must
when they buy killers
when they arm them
when they enter our homes
chanting and jumping
singing and ready to kill
come and be with me
come with a fight in your heart
come
let them come eyeball to eyeball with justice
come
come and be with me
in the early hours
in the thick of night
in broad daylight
when they bring death to our doorstep
you and i must be there

they have now started under the bright sky of
   Magaliesberg
and in Natal
in the green and lush and tall sugar cane
under the sticky heat of mirage
and into the townships of Johannesburg
and on the plain and vastness of the Free State
they dip the spears and wash the pangas
they clean their guns
we carry the dead or cover them in newspapers

which wear startling headlines
in ravines
in the streets
in flats
in shacks
in cars
in trains and in taxis
men women and children lie dead
we dig holes and live in burials
we are used to funerals

my countrymen and women
did we not sing and dance
did we not aspire
did we not engrave in our hearts and minds
in the early hours of the morning and in the deep of
    night
in the sun glittering day
did we
did we not
with life and death ring the air with a clarion call
for life
for knowledge
for something to eat and to drink
for the right to plan and to build
for a land and a country
did we not give life
did we
did we not give sons and daughters
were we not ready to give and to offer all we have and
    had
for all to our land
did we

did we not aspire and return
when we sang
when we danced and chanted
entering civilisation

when we called on history and held it in our hand
entering it like an elephant a bush
and called on some men and women of our country
those who had gone insane
because they are white
did we
did we not

so here we are
again
mad men and women
the white and the tribal ask us
did we
in that day and in that life
did we not live in dreams and desire
in hope and belief
even when the day crushed and popped our time
turning the sky crimson and the night cast upon us
dark and cold shadows
and the sky, stern, hovered above us
did we

did we not live in dreams and hopes
strong we stared death in the eye for love of life
remember
we agreed with civilisation
we agreed with history
that yes when history repeats itself
as do the sea waves
flowing and climbing and ebbing
they ride and roll
with time and the seasons
in them we
men and women create with and mould nature
to let live

we must
in history when it repeats itself

we will create with and mould it
to let live, we shall return
in the early hours of the morning
in the deep of night and at high noon

so
in the night
and in the day
against the steep and slope of history
here we are again
we hold on to the memory and the old story
that life must be lived
history when it repeats itself
must bend and fold and knot
as we shape it for life
we do not need a civil war

come my countrymen
come and dream and hope with me
we must oh Africa
surge

we must
shine the blade of the spear against the sun and the moon
for peace
we must return
to the African heart
to the spirit whose dignity stood the pain and humiliation
of poverty
when oppression like a whip
larded every inch of our flesh
and cracked in every nerve of our life

when history repeats itself
let's deliver humanness to the knowledge of humanbeings
come
and hope and dream with me
when we prepare for war for peace

come with a fight in your heart
come with truth
come with knowledge for life
come and be with me

we must return
like the sun and the moon
like the seasons
to replenish life for it to be lived
we do not need any civil wars when history repeats itself
in life
we must return
with time with the seasons with history
like the sea waves when they climb and fall and ebb
we must return
inside history and with it
ah Africa
what have the multitudes not built
what is it they are not ready for
come
come and see their eyes and faces
come and touch their hard hands
come and hear their voices
come and listen
come and be with us in the day and the night
come and take hope with you
because here you will know those tales which incriminate
come
if the truth does stalk us
we will befriend wisdom
you and i
come
let us return
come
come and be with me
come and hope and dream with me when the dream
    dawns.

28